THE WAY TO NIBBANA

By VEN. NARADA THERA

Published by

THE BUDDHIST MISSIONARY SOCIETY,
JALAN BERHALA, KUALA LUMPUR 09-06,
MALAYSIA.

ABOUT THIS BOOK

Nibbana or *Nirvana* can be interpreted to mean the extinction of the thirst for sensual pleasures. Many people are under the impression that they could find eternal peace and happiness by providing themselves more and more things to satisfy their own senses. But this would be an endless job. The more we give the more they want. Therefore no one could fulfil the eternal thirst of the senses forever. Man may work as hard as a slave up to his last breath to satisfy them; yet he will die without his sensual thirst satisfied. His desire or thirst will continue to prevail in him even though he is not in a position to make use of his faculties.

The infallible method to quench this thirst as introduced by the Buddha is to calm down the senses instead of gratifying them. To do this, man has to understand the real nature of this life and the universal laws. He must have the courage not to become a slave to his senses. He must learn how to control his senses and the mind through self-training, discipline and restraint. He must learn to achieve contentment and detachment. Very few people have realised that the cause of suffering is due to their own attachment and craving towards various things. They are not in a position to understand that some day they might have to depart from everything they now hold so dear in this world.

The Buddhist *Nibbana* is quite different from the paradise introduced by other religions. The Buddhist way of salvation and eternal bliss cannot be obtained unless man purifies himself by becoming a perfect one. But followers of other faiths believe that they can find their salvation through the influence of God, by praying to and believing in Him.

i

Buddhists also believe that there are certain heavenly abodes for good people who have done some meritorious deeds, to enjoy their sensual pleasures; but in such places no one could find eternal bliss but only temporary happiness, for one day there will be an end to such pleasures. According to Buddhism, heaven is not a place where man can get rid of the Cycle of Birth and Death. For as long as he has the craving for sensual pleasures, he will continue to be subjected to birth and death.

There is a great difference between the pleasure one derives from sensual gratification and that which one gets from restraining from it. Thus it was the Buddha who taught for the first time that the highest form of bliss in life is to be attained by controlling one's senses and not by indulging in them freely. While some religions say that beings attain immortality after death, others proclaim that there is no life after death. According to Buddhism, however, both these views are unacceptable. All changes in life are due to the good and bad actions of the individual. One is not free from suffering so long as he is subjected to defilements.

Unless and until one becomes a perfect man by annihilating all his defilements or corruptions, he will not be free from decay, sickness, worries and other encumbrances.

People are forever struggling in this world trying to find peace and happiness by adopting various erroneous methods not knowing of the real path because of their own ignorance.

It is very clear that according to Buddhism no one can expect to obtain salvation or eternal bliss simply by praying to a god or by performing ceremonies, rites and rituals. To obtain that, one must be good to oneself and to others as well. He has to cultivate himself by observing certain precepts, by abstaining from evil and by purifying his mind. Nobody else can purify man by washing away all his sins or evil. Man must do that for himself.

"*Nibbana* can never be explained completely and satisfactorily in words, because our language is too inadequate to express or describe the real nature of the Absolute Truth or ultimate Reality which is *Nibbana*. Language is created and used by the masses of human beings to express things and ideas as experienced by their sense organs and their mind. Supramundane experience like that of the Absolute Truth does not come under such a category. Words are symbols representing things and ideas known to us, but these symbols do not and cannot fully convey the true nature of even ordinary things. Language is considered deceptive and misleading in the matter of understanding of the Truth. Nevertheless we cannot do without language. But if *Nibbana* is to be expressed and explained in positive terms, we are immediately likely to grasp an idea generally associated with those terms, which may be quite the contrary. Therefore it is generally expressed in negative terms – a less dangerous move perhaps. So it is often referred to by such negative terms as "Extinction of Thirst, uncompound, unconditioned, absence of desire, cessation, blowing out, or extinctive".

It is the complete cessation of that very thirst, giving it up, renouncing it, emancipation and detachment from it.

"Calming of all conditioned things, giving up all defilements" *Nibbana* is thus expressed in negative terms. There are many who have got a wrong notion that it is negative, and expresses self-annihilation. *Nibbana* is definitely no annihilation of self, because there is no self to annihilate. If at all, it is the annihilation of the illusion, of the false idea of self.

Buddhism holds that final extinction of ignorance is the way of escape from the wheel of life, but the escape is not reached, and of course, in the Buddhist system, could not be reached, in a union with Brahma or God which is to be attained only in an after-life. The victory to be gained by the liquidation of ignorance, in the Buddha's view, is a victory which can be gained and enjoyed in this life itself. This is what is meant by the Buddhist ideal of Arahantship – the life of a man made perfect by insight, the life of a man who has travelled along the Noble Eightfold Path and broken all the Fetters, and carried out, in its entirety, the Buddhist system of self-culture and self-control.

This transcedent life, the Buddha maintains, can be normally obtained before the bodily death of man, and he equates it to happiness of the highest order, accompanied too by consciousness of the destruction of individualistic desire or selfhood. In this transcendental absolute entity, man loses consciousness of his separate self and dissolves into the Nibbanic state. Then man becomes the very embodiment of the Ten Perfections or *Paramitas* of Liberality (dana), Morality (sila), Renunciation (nekkhamma), Wisdom (panna), Energy (viriya), Forgiveness (khanti), Truthfulness (sacca), Resolution (adhitthana), Love (metta), and Equanimity (upekkha).

The transition is from an egoistic life to one of self-forgetfulness, an inward peace which could never be shaken. Those who had reached this state, could be able to enjoy the peace of mental condition. There are an endless number of names attached to such a state each based on one of the phases of the many-sided whole, namely Emancipation, the Island of Refuge, the End of Craving, the State of Purity, the Supreme, the Transcendent, the Tranquil, the Unchanging, the Goingout, the Unshaken, the Imperishable, the Ambrosia, and so on. One epithet is however more familiar and this is *Nibbana*, "the Going-out" that is to say, the going-out in the heart, of three fires of greed, hatred and delusion.

Greed, hatred, and delusion are called "the three fires", the extinction of which leads to the state of the *Arahat*, the man who has attained *Nibbana*. As the literal meaning of the word *Nibbana* is "Going-out" or "extinction", it might cause some to presume that the word is synonymous with "annihilation". But *Nibbana* really means the higher·life of the man who has risen above himself. It means the extinction of the illusion of self, and the consequent annihilation of selfishness. It is the state of complete enlightenment, of perfect goodness, and of perfect peace. The Buddha compares it to a "city of peace". It is incorrect to say that *Nibbana* is negative or positive. The ideas of "negative" and "positive" are relative, and are within the realm of reality. These terms cannot be applied to *Nibbana* the Absolute Truth, which is beyond duality and relativity.

Here in this book Ven Narada Maha Thera, a learned Buddhist scholar, author of many Buddhist books and also a well-known Buddhist Missionary, has given us some valuable ideas and introduced to us the method to be practised, as was taught by the Buddha to achieve permanent peace and happiness. By following this method one can certainly achieve this final goal or the purpose of life in order to end the unsatisfactoriness of this life.

Sincere thanks and appreciation are due to Ven. Narada Maha Thera for contributing valuable articles for this book and to Datin Gladys Loke Chua for her kind donation made towards the cost of printing this book in memory of her beloved husband, the late Dato Dr. Chua Sin Kah.

MAY YOU ALL ATTAIN PEACE AND HAPPINESS.

K. Dhammananda

Buddhist Temple
Jalan Berhala
Kuala Lumpur
Malaysia.

THE WAY TO NIBBANA

THE SUBLIME STATES

Rare is birth as a human being
Hard is the life of mortals
Do not let slip this opportunity.

Dhammapada

Man is a mysterious being with inconceivable potentialities. Latent in him are both saintly characteristics and criminal tendency. They may rise to the surface at unexpected moments in disconcerting strength. How they orginated we know not. We only know that they are dormant in man in varying degree.

Within the powerful mind in this complex of man are also found a store house of virtues and a rubbish heap of evil. With the development of the respective characteristics, man may become either a blessing or a curse to humanity.

Those who wish to be great, noble, and serviceable, who wish to sublimate themselves and serve humanity both by example and by precept, and who wish to avail themselves of this golden opportunity as human beings, endeavour their best to remove the latent vices and to cultivate the dormant virtues.

To dig up precious gems embedded in the earth, men spend enormous sums of money and make laborious efforts, and sometimes even sacrifice their lives. But to dig up the valuable treasures latent in man, only persistent effort and

1

enduring patience are necessary. Even the poorest man or woman can accomplish this task; for wealth is not an essential prerequisite to the accumulation of transendental treasures.

It is strange that the vices latent in man seem to be almost natural and spontaneous. It is equally strange that every vice possesses its opposite sterling virtue, which does not however appear to be so normal and automatic, though still within the range of all.

One powerful destructive vice in man is anger. The sweet virtue that subdues this evil force and sublimates man is loving-kindness (metta).

Cruelty is another vice that is responsible for many errors and atrocities prevalent in the world. Compassion is its antidote.

Jealousy is another vice that poisons one's systems and leads to unhealthy rivalries and dangerous competitions. The most effective remedy for this poisonous drug is appreciative joy.

There are two other universal characteristics that upset the mental equipoise of man. They are attachment to the pleasurable and aversion to the non-pleasurable. These two opposite forces can be eliminated by developing equanimity.

These four sterling virtues are collectively termed in Pali Brahmavihara which may be rendered by Modes of Sublime Conduct, Sublime States, or Divine Abodes.

These virtues tend to elevate man. They make one

divine in this life itself. They can transform man into a superman. If all try to cultivate them irrespective of creed, colour, race, or sex, the earth can be transformed into a paradise where all can live in perfect peace and harmony as ideal citizens of one world.

The four sublime virtues are also termed illimitables. They are so called because they find no barrier or limit and should be extended towards all beings without exception. They embrace all living beings including animals.

Irrespective of religious beliefs, one can cultivate these sweet virtues and be a blessing to oneself and all others.

METTA

The first Sublime State is *Metta.* It means that which softens one's heart or the state of a true friend. It is defined as the sincere wish for the welfare and genuine happiness of all living beings without exception. It is also explained as the friendly disposition, for a genuine friend sincerely wishes for the welfare of his friend.

Just as a mother protects her only child even at the risk of her life, even so one should cultivate boundless-kindness towards all living beings, is the advice of the Buddha.

It is not the passionate love of the mother towards her child that is stressed here but her sincere wish for the genuine welfare of her child.

Metta is neither carnal love nor personal affection, for grief inevitably arises from both.

Metta is not neighbourliness, for it makes no distinction between neighbours and others.

Metta is not mere universal brotherhood, for it embraces all living beings including animals, lesser brethren and sisters that need greater compassion as they are helpless.

Metta is not political brotherhood or racial brotherhood, or national brotherhood, or even religious brotherhood.

Political brotherhood is confined only to those who share similar political views, such as the partial brotherhood of Democrats, Socialists, Communists, and so forth.

Racial brotherhood and national brotherhood are restricted only to those of the same race and nation. Some nationalists love their race so much that sometimes they ruthlessly kill innocent men, women and children because they unfortunately are not blessed with blond hair and blue eyes. The white races have a particular love for the white skin, the black for the balck, the yellow for the yellow, the brown for the brown, the pale for the pale, the red for the red. Others of a different complexion are at times viewed with suspicion and fear. Very often to assert their racial superiority they resort to brutal warfare, killing millions by mercilessly raining bombs from the sky above. The pathetic incidents of the Second World War are striking examples which can never be forgotten by mankind.

Amongst some narrow-minded peoples, within the wider circles of their ancient nations, there exist minor circles of caste and class where the so-called brotherhood of the powerful oppressors is so limited that the oppressed are not even permitted to enjoy bare human rights merely because of the accidents of birth or class. These oppressors are to be pitied because they are confined to their water-tight compartments.

Metta is not religious brotherhood either. Owing to the sad limitations of so-called religious brotherhood, human heads have been severed without the least compunctions, sincere outspoken men and women have been roasted and burnt alive; many atrocities have been perpetrated which baffle description; cruel wars have been waged which mar the pages of world history. Even in this supposedly enlightened twentieth century, the followers of one religion hate or ruthlessly persecute and even kill those of other faiths merely because they cannot force them to think as they do or because they have a different label.

If, on account of religious views, people of different faiths cannot meet on a common platform like brothers and sisters, then surely the missions of compassionate world teachers have pitifully failed.

Sweet *Metta* transcends all these kinds of narrow brotherhood. It is limitless in scope and range. Barriers it has none. Discrimination it makes not. *Metta* enables one to regard the whole world as one's motherland and all as fellow-beings.

Just as the sun sheds its ray on all without any distinction, even so sublime *Metta* bestows its sweet blessings equally on the pleasant and the unpleasant, on the rich and the poor, on the high and the low, on the vicious and the virtuous, on man and woman, and on human animals.

5

Such was the boundless *Metta* of the Buddha who worked for the welfare and happiness of those who loved Him as well as of those who hated Him and even attempted to harm and kill Him.

The Buddha exercised *Metta* equally towards His own son Rahula, His adversary Devadatta, His attendant Ananda, His admirers and His opponents.

This loving-kindness should be extended in equal measure towards oneself as towards friend, foe and neutral alike. Suppose a bandit were to approach a person travelling through a forest with an intimate friend, a neutral person and an enemy, and suppose he were to demand that one of them be offered as a victim. If the traveller were to say that he himself should be taken, then he would have no *Metta* towards himself. If he were to say that anyone of the other three persons should be taken, then he would have no *Metta* towards them.

Such is the characteristic of real *Metta*. In exercising this boundless loving-kindness, oneself should not be ignored. This subtle point should not be misunderstood, for self-sacrifice is another sweet virtue and egolessness is yet another higher virtue. The culmination of this *Metta* is the identification of oneself with all beings making no difference between oneself and others. The so-called 'I' is lost in the whole. Separatism evaporates. Oneness is realized.

There is no proper English equivalent for this graceful Pali term *Metta*. Goowill, loving-kindness, benevolence and universal love are suggested as the best renderings.

The antithesis of *Metta* is anger, illwill, hatred, or aver-

6

sion. *Metta* cannot co-exist with anger or vengeful conduct.

Metta not only tends to conquer anger but also does not tolerate hateful thoughts towards others. He who has *Metta* never thinks of harming others, nor does he disparage or condemn others. Such a person is neither afraid of others nor does he instill fear into any.

A subtle indirect enemy assails *Metta* in the guise of a friend. It is selfish affection for unguarded *Metta* may sometimes be assailed by lust. This indirect enemy resembles a person who lurks afar in the jungles or hills to cause harm to another. Grief springs from affection but not from *Metta*.

This delicate point should not be misunderstood. Parents surely cannot avoid having affection towards their children and children towards their parents; husbands towards their wives and wives towards their husbands. Such affection is quite natural. The world cannot exist without mutual affection. The point to be clarified here is that unselfish *Metta* is not synonymous with ordinary affection.

A benevolent attitude is the chief characteristic of *Metta*. He who practises *Metta* is constantly interested in promoting the welfare of others. He seeks the good and beautiful in all but the ugliness in others.

ATTENDANT BLESSINGS OF METTA

1. He who practises *Metta* sleeps happily. As he goes to sleep with a light heart free from hatred, he naturally falls asleep at once. This fact is clearly demonstrated by those who are full of loving-kindness. They are fast asleep imme-

diately on closing their eyes.

2.   As he goes to sleep with a loving heart, he awakes with an equally loving heart. Benevolent and compassionate persons often rise from bed with smiling faces.

3.   Even in sleep, loving persons are not perturbed by bad dreams. As they are full of love during their waking hours, they are peaceful in their sleeping hours too. Either they fall into deep sleep or have pleasant dreams.

4.   He becomes dear to human beings. As he loves others, so do others love him.

When a person looks to a mirror with a smiling face, a similar face will greet him If, on the contrary, he looks with a wry face, he will see a similar reflection. The outside world reacts on one in the same way that one acts towards the world. One full of faults himself is apt to see the evil in others. The good he ignores.

Why should we see the ugliness in others when there is evil in the best of us and good in the worst of us? It would be a source of pleasure to all, if we could see the good and beautiful in all.

5.   He who practises *Metta* is dear to non-human as well. Animals are also attracted to him. Radiating their loving-kindness, ascetics live in wild forests amidst ferocious beasts without being harmed by them.

6.   Owing to his power of *Metta,* he becomes immune from poison and so forth unless he is subjected to some inexorable *Kamma*.

As *Metta* is a constructive healthy force, it has the power to counteract hostile influences. Just as hateful thoughts can produce toxic effects in the system, even so loving thoughts can produce healthy physical effects.

When the Buddha visited His birthplace for the first time, His son Rahula, who was only seven years of age, approached Him and spontaneously remarked: O ascetic, even your shadow is pleasing to me. The child was so much dominated by the Buddha's *Metta* that he deeply felt its magnetic power.

7. Invisible deities protect him because of the power of his *Metta*.

8. *Metta* leads to quick mental concentration. As the mind is not perturbed by hostile vibrations, one-pointedness can be gained with ease. With mind at peace he will live in heaven of his own creation. Even those who come in contact with him will also experience that bliss.

9. *Metta* tends to beautify one's facial expression. The face as a rule reflects the state of mind. When one gets angry, the heart pumps blood twice or three times faster than the normal rate. Heated blood rushes up to the face, which then turns red or black. At such times, the face becomes repulsive to sight. Loving thoughts, on the contrary, gladden the heart and clarify the blood. The face then presents a loveable appearance.

It is stated that when the Buddha, after Englightenment, reflected on the Causal Relations (Patthana), his heart was so pacified and His blood yellow, red, white, orange, and a mixture of these emanated from His body.

10. A person imbued with *Metta* dies peacefully as he harbours no thoughts of hatred towards any. Even after death, his serene face reflects his peaceful death.

11. Since a person with *Metta* dies happily, he will subsequently be born in a blissful state. If he gained the *Jhanas* (ecstasies), he will be born in a Brahma realm.

POWER OF METTA

Besides these inevitable worldly blessings *Metta* possesses a magnetic power. It can produce a good influence on others even at a distance and can attract others to oneself.

Once an intoxicated elephant was driven towards the Buddha in an effort to kill Him. The Buddha calmly radiated His love towards the elephant and subdued it.

A beautiful story may be cited to show how the Bodhisatta as a boy extended his boundless *Metta* when his own father ordered him to be killed. Young though he was, the Bodhisatta thought to himself:—

"Here is a golden opportunity for me to practise my *Metta*. My father stands before me, my good mother is weeping, the executioner is ready to chop of my hands and feet. I, the victim, am in the centre. Love I must all the four in equal measure without any distinction. May my good father not incur suffering because of this ruthless act! May I become a Buddha in the future!"

In one of his previous births the Bodhisatta was once practising the virtue of patience in a royal park. The king, a drunkard, meant to test his patience. The impatient king kicked him and cut off his hands and feet. Still he practised patience. The impatient king kicked him in the chest. Lying in a pool of blood, almost on the verge of death, the Bodhisatta blessed the king and wished him long life saying that men like himself never get angry.

The Buddha Himself has set the noble example: "As an elephant in the battlefield withstands arrows shot from a bow," says the Buddha, "even so will I endure abuse: verily most people are undisciplined."

This chaotic, war weary, restless world of today, where the nations are arming themselves to their teeth, frightened of one another, where human life is endangered by nuclear weapons which may be released at any moment, is surely in need of this universal loving kindness so that all may live in one world in perfect peace and harmony like brothers and sisters.

Is it practically possible to exercise *Metta* when one is threatened with devastating bombs and other destructive weapons?

Well, what can powerless people do when bombs rain from above? Can they avert such a catastrophe?

Buddhist *Metta* is the only answer to such deadly bombs when one is faced with inexorable death.

If all warlike nations could be prevailed upon to substitute this spiritual *Metta* for the destructive weapons of materialism and rule the world not with might and force but with right and love, then only would there be genuine peace and happiness in this world.

Leaving the almost practical major issues aside, it is advisable to be concerned with oneself and the rest of mankind in cultivating this sweet virtue of *Metta* to the best of one's ability

HOW TO PRACTISE METTA

A few practical hints are given below to practise this meditation on loving-kindness.

Metta should be practised first towards oneself. In doing so a person should charge his mind and body with positive thoughts of peace and happiness. He should think how he could be peaceful, happy, free from suffering, worry and anger. He becomes ever to learn and tries his best not to give occasion for anger to arise. By loving-kindness, he cuts off all hostile vibrations and negative thoughts. He returns good for evil, love for anger. He becomes ever tolerant and tries his best not to give occasion for anger to any. Himself beaming with happiness, he injects happiness into others not only inwardly but also outwardly by putting his *Metta* into practice in the course of his daily life.

When he is full of peace and is free from thoughts of hatred, it is easy for him to radiate loving-kindness towards others. What he does not possess, he cannot give to others. Before he tries to make others happy, he should first be happy himself. He should know the ways and means to make himself happy.

He now radiates his loving-kindness towards all his near

12

and dear ones individually and collectively, wishing them peace and happiness and freedom from suffering, disease, worry and anger.

Diffusing his thoughts of loving-kindness towards his relatives and friends, he radiates them also towards neturals. Just as he wished for the dear ones even so he sincerely wishes for the peace and happiness of those who are neutral to him, wishing them freedom from suffering, disease, worry and anger. Finally, though this is somewhat difficult, he should radiate his *Metta* in the same way towards those (if any) who are inimical to him. If by practising *Metta,* he could adopt a friendly attitude towards those thought to be inimical towards him, his achievement would be more heroic and commendable. As the Buddha advises — (Admist those who hate, let him live free from hatred).

Starting from himself he should gradually extend his *Metta* towards all beings, irrespective of creed, colour, or sex, including dumb animals, until he had identified himself with all, making no distinction whatever. He merges himself in the whole universe and is one with all. He is no more dominated by egotistic feelings. He transcends all forms of separatism. No longer confining himself to water-tight compartments, no longer influenced by caste, class, national, racial, or religious prejudices, he can regard the whole world as his motherland and all as fellow-beings in the ocean of life.

KARUNA

The second virtue that sublimates man is compassion (karuna). It is defined as that which makes the hearts of the good quiver when others are subjected to suffering, or that which dissipates the sufferings of others. Its chief characteristic is the wish to remove the woes of others.

The hearts of compassionate persons are even softer than flowers. They do not and cannot rest satisfied until they relieve the sufferings of others. At times they even go to the extent of sacrificing their lives so as to alleviate the sufferings of others. The story of the *Vyaghri Jataka* where the Bodhisatta sacrificed his life to save a starving tigress and her cubs may be citied as an example.

It is compassion that compels one to serve others with altruistic motives. A truly compassionate person lives not for himself but for others. He seeks opportunities to serve others expecting nothing in return, not even gratitude.

WHO NEED COMPASSION?

Many amidst us deserve our compassion. The poor and the needy, the sick and the helpless, the lonely and the destitute, the ignorant and the vicious, the impure and the undisciplined are some that demand the compassion of kindhearted, noble-minded men and women, to whatever religion or to whatever race they belong.

Some countries are materially rich but spiritually poor while some others are spiritually rich but materially poor. Both these pathetic conditions have to be taken into consideration by the materially rich and the spiritually rich.

It is the paramount duty of the wealthy to come to the succour of the poor, who unfortunately lack most of the necessaries of life. Surely those who have in abundance can give to the poor and the needy their surplus without inconveniencing themselves.

Once a young student removed the door curtain in his house and gave it to a poor person telling his good mother that the door does not feel the cold but the poor certainly do. Such a kind-hearted attitude in young men and women is highly commendable.

It is gratifying to note that some wealthy countries have formed themselves into various philanthropic bodies to help under-developed countries, especially in Asia, in every possible way. Charitable organizations have also been established in all countries by men, women and students to give every possible assistance to the poor and the needy. Religious bodies also perform their respective duties in this connection in their own humble way. Homes for the Aged, Orphanages and other similar charitable institutions are needed in under-developed countries.

The beggar problem has still to be solved in some countries where begging has become a profession. Out of compassion for the unfortunate beggars, this problem has to be solved satisfactorily by the respective Governments as the existence of beggars is an insult to any self-respecting nation.

As the materially rich should have compassion on the materially poor and try to elevate them, it is a duty of the spiritually rich, too, to have compassion on the spiritually poor and sublimate them though they may be materially rich. Wealth alone cannot give genuine happiness. Peace of mind can be gained not by material treasures but by spiritual treasures. Many in this world are badly in need of substantial spiritual food which is not easily obtained as the spiritually poor far exceed the materially poor numerically as they are found both amongst the rich and the poor.

Even more than poverty, sickness prevails throughout the world. Many are physically sick, some are mentally sick. Science provides effective medicine for the former but not the latter, who very often languish in mental hospitals.

There are causes for these two kinds of diseases. Compassionate men and women must try to remove the causes if they wish to produce an effective cure.

Effective measures have been employed by various nations to prevent and cure diseases not only of mankind but also of animals.

The Buddha set a noble example by attending on the sick Himself and exhorting His disciples with the memorable words: "He who ministers unto the sick ministers unto me."

Some selfless doctors render free services towards the alleviation of suffering. Some expend their whole time and energy in ministering to the poor patients even at the risk of their lives.

Hospitals and free dispensaries have become a blessing to humanity but more are needed so that the poor may benefit by them. In undeveloped countries, the poor suffer through lack of medical facilities. The sick have to be carried for miles with great inconvenience to the nearest hospital or dispensary for medical treatment. Sometimes they die on the way. Pregnant mothers suffer most. Hospitals, dispensaries, maternity homes, etc. are essential needs in backward village areas.

The lowly and the destitute deserve the compassion of wealthy men and women. Sometimes servants and workers are not well paid, well fed, well clothed and more often than not they are illtreated. Justice is not meted out to them. They are neglected and are powerless as there is nobody to plead for them. Glaring cases of inhuman cruelty receive publicity in some exceptional cases. Many such cases are not known. These unfortunate ones have no other alternative but to suffer meekly even as Mother earth suffers everything in silence. When the grief is unbearable, they commit suicide in utter desperation.

The vicious, the wicked, and the ignorant deserve compassion even more than those who suffer physically as they are metally and spiritually sick. They should not be condemned and despised but sympathised with for their failings and defects. Though a mother has equal compassion towards all her children, still she may have more compassion towards a sick child. Even so greater compassion should be exercised towards the spiritually sick as their sickness ruins their character.

The Buddha, for instance, has great compassion towards the courtesan Ambapali, and towards Angulimala the murderer both of whom later became His converts and underwent a complete reformation in character.

We must understand that greatness is latent in all however wicked they may be. Perhaps one appropriate word at the right moment may change the whole outlook of a person.

The Emperor Asoka perpetrated many crimes, so much so that he was stigmatized Asoka the Wicked. Later the words from a young novice "Diligence is the path to the deathless" produced such a great change in him that he became Asoka the Righteous.

The Buddha's advice is to shun the company of the foolish. That does not mean that the good should not associate with them so as to reform them. People avoid those who suffer from contagious diseases. But compassionate physicians attend on them so as to heal them. Otherwise they might die. In the same way, the wicked may die spiritually if the good are not tolerant and compassionate towards them.

As a rule Buddha went in search of the poor, the ignorant and the vicious, but the good and the virtuous came in search of the Buddha.

Like *Metta* (loving-kindness), *Karuna* (compassion) should also be extended without limit towards all suffering and helpless beings, including dumb animals born and unborn.

To deny the rights and privileges of mankind on account of caste, colour, or race is inhuman and cruel. To feast on the flesh of animals by passion, to rain bombs from above and ruthlessly destroy millions of men, women and children is the worst form of cruelty that deluded man has ever perpetrated.

Today this pitiless, vengeful world has sacrified the most precious things on earth-life at the altar of brute force. Whither has compassion fled?

The world needs today compassionate men and women to banish violence and cruelty from the face of the earth.

Buddhist compassion, it should be noted, does not consist in mere shedding of tears and the like, for the indirect enemy of compassion is passionate grief.

Compassion embraces all sorrow-stricken beings, while loving-kindness embraces all living beings, happy or sorrowful.

MUDITA

The third sublime virtue is *Mudita*. It is not mere sympathy but sympathetic or appreciative joy which tends to destroy jealousy, its direct enemy.

One devastating force that endangers our whole constitution is jealousy. Very often some cannot bear to see or hear the successful achievement of others. They rejoice over their failures but cannot tolerate their successes. Instead of praising and congratulating the successful, they try to ruin, condemn and vilify them. In one way, *Mudita* is concerned more with oneself than with others as it tends to eradicate jealousy which ruins oneself. On the other hand, it aids others as well since one who practises *Mudita* will not try to hinder the progress and welfare of others.

As it is with loving-kindness, it is easy to rejoice over the success of one's near and dear ones but rather difficult to do so over the success of one's adversaries. Yes, the majority not only find it difficult but also do not and cannot rejoice. They seek delight in creating every possible obstacle so as to ruin their adversaries.

They even go to the extent of poisoning, crucifying, and

assassinating the good.

Socrates was poisoned, Christ was crucified, Gandhi was shot. Such is the nature of the wicked and deluded world.

The practice of *Metta* and *Karuna* is easier than the practice of *Mudita*, which demands great personal effort and strong will-power.

Do the Western nations rejoice over the prosperity of the Eastern and the Eastern over the prosperity of the Western? Does one nation rejoice over the welfare of another nation? Is one race happy over the growing prosperity of another race? Does even one religious sect, which stands for the cultivation of morals, rejoice over the spiritual influence of another sect?

One religion is jealous of another religion, one part of of the globe is jealous of another part of the globe, one institution is jealous of another institution, one business firm is jealous of another business firm, one family is jealous of another family, unsuccessful pupils are jealous of successful pupils, sometimes even one brother or sister is jealous of another brother or sister.

This is the very reason why individuals and groups should practise sympathetic joy if they wish to sublimate themselves and be internally happy.

The chief characteristic of *Mudita* is happy acquiescence in others' prosperity and success. Laughter and the like are not the characteristics of *Mudita* as exhilaration is regarded as its indirect enemy.

Mudita embraces all prosperous beings and is the congratulatory attitude of a person. It tends to eliminate any dislike towards a successful person.

UPEKKHA

The fourth sublime state is the most difficult and the most essential. It is *Upekkha* or equanimity. The etymological meaning of the term *Upekkha* is discerning rightly, viewing justly or looking impartially, that is without attachment or aversion, without favour or disfavour.

Equanimity is necessary, especially for laymen who have to live in an ill-balanced world amidst fluctuating circumstances.

Slights and insults are the common lot of mankind. The world is so constituted that the good and the virtuous are often subjected to unjust criticism and attack. It is heroic to maintain a balanced mind in such circumstances.

Loss and gain, fame and infamy, praise and blame, pain and happiness are eight worldly conditions that affect all humanity. Most people are perturbed when affected by such favourable or unfavourable states. One is elated when one is praised, and depressed when blamed and reviled. He is wise, says the Buddha, who, admist such vicissitudes of life, stand unmoved like unto a firm rock, exercising perfect equanimity.

The Buddha's examplary life offers us worldlings an excellent example of equanimity.

There was no religious teacher in the world who was so severely criticised, attacked, insulted and reviled as the Buddha, and yet none so highly praised, honoured and revered as the Buddha.

Once when He went in quest of alms, He was called an outcaste by an impertinent Brahmin. He calmly endured the insult and explained to him that it is not birth that makes one an outcaste but an ignoble character. The Brahmin was converted.

Inviting Him to a house for alms, a certain man entertained the Buddha with the filthiest language current in His time. He was called 'swine', 'brute', 'ox' etc. But he was not offended. He did not retaliate. Calmly He questioned His host what he would do when guests visited his house. He replied that he would prepare a feast to entertain them.

"Well, what would you do if they did not partake of it?" questioned the Buddha.

"In that case, we ourselves would partake of the feast."

"Well, good brother, you have invited me to your house for alms. You have entertained me with a torrent of abuse. I do not accept it. Please take it back," calmly replied the Buddha. The offender's character was completely transformed.

"Retaliate not. Be silent as a cracked gong when you are abused by others. If you do so, I deem that you have already attained *Nibbana* although you have not realized *Nibbana.*" Such is the advice of the Buddha.

These are golden words that should be given heed to in this ill-disciplined world of today.

Once a lady of the court induced some drunkards to revile the Buddha so much that venerable Ananda, His attendant disciple, implored the Buddha to leave the city and go elsewhere. But the Buddha was unperturbed.

Another woman feigned pregnancy and publicly accused the Buddha of having placed her in that condition. A woman was killed by His rivals and the Buddha was accused of murder. His own cousin and disciple Devadatta made an unsuccessful attempt to crush Him to death by hurling a rock from a cliff. Some of His own disciple accused Him of jealousy, partiality, favouritism, etc.

On the other hand, many sang the praises of the Buddha. Kings prostrated themselves before His feet and paid the highest reverence.

Like the Mother Earth, the Buddha suffered everything in silence with perfect equanimity.

Like a lion that does not tremble at every sound, one should not be perturbed by the poisoned darts of uncurbed tongues. Like the wind that does not cling to the meshes of a net, one should not be attached to the illusory pleasures of this changing world. Like the lotus that is unsoiled by the mud from which it springs, one should live unaffected by worldly temptations, ever calm, serene and peaceful.

Metta embraces all beings, *Karuna* embraces sufferers, *Mudita* embraces the prosperous, and *Upekkha* embraces the good and the bad, the loved and the unloved, the pleasant

23

and the unpleasant.

He who wishes to be divine in this life itself may daily cultivate these four sublime virtues which are dormant in all.

He who wishes to perfect himself and compassionately work for the welfare of all beings in the course of his countless births in *samsara* may strenuously develop the ten Perfections (Parami) and ultimately become a *Samma Sambuddha,* a Supremely Enlightened One.

He who wishes to eradicate his passions and put an end to suffering by realizing *Nibbana* at the earliest possible opportunity may diligently follow the unique Noble Eightfold Path which still exists in its pristine purity.

The Buddha exhorts:—

"Suppose, O monks, this mighty earth were one mass of water, and a man were to throw down thereon a yoke with one hole. Then comes a wind from the east and wafts it west amd a wind from the west and wafts it east; a north wind wafts it south, and a south wind wafts it north. Then once at the end of a hundred years, a turtle blind in one eye pushed his neck through that yoke with one hole when he popped up to the surface at the end of a hundred years."

"It is difficult, Lord, that that turtle would do that," said the monks.

"It is just as difficult, O monks that one will get birth in human form just as difficult that a Tathagata should arise in the world, an Arahat, a fully Enlightened One; just as difficult that the Norm (Dhamma) and Disciple (Vinaya) proclaimed by a Tathagata should be shown in the world.

But now indeed, O monk, this state of human birth is won, and a Tathagata has arisen in the world, and the Norm and Discipline proclaimed by the Tathagata is shown in the world.

Wherefore, O monks, ye must make an effort to realize: This is ill, this is the cause of ill, this is the cessation of ill, this is the way leading to the cessation of ill.

_____

THE WAY TO NIBBANA (I)

"This Middle Path leads to tranquility, realization, enlightenment and *Nibbana*."

Dhamma Chakka Sutta

MORALITY

The way to *Nibbana* is the Middle Path which avoids the extreme of self-mortification that weakens the intellect and the extreme of self-indulgence that retards moral progress.

This Middle Path consists of the following eight factors: Right Understanding, Right Thoughts, Right Speech, Right Action, Right Livelihood, Right Effort, Right Mindfulness, and Right Concentration.

The first two are classified as Wisdom (panna), the second three as Morality (sila), and the last three as Concentration (samadhi).

According to the order of development Morality, Concentration, and Wisdom are the three stages on the Grand Highway that leads to *Nibbana*.

These three stages are embodied in that beautiful ancient verse:

Sabba papassa akaranam — Kusalassa upasampada
Sacittapariyodapanam — etam Buddhana sasanam

To cease from all evil

To cultivate good
To purify one's mind—
This is the advice of all the Buddhas.

We reap what we sow. Evil results in pain, and good in happiness. Our pain and happiness are the direct results of our own good and evil.

A person with a right understanding realizes this just law of action and reaction and, of his own accord, refrains from evil and does good to the best of his ability. He does so for his own good and for the good of others. He considers it his duty to live as a blessing to himself and to all others.

Knowing that life is precious to all as that none has any right whatever to destroy the life of another, he extends compassion and loving-kindness towards every living being, even to the tiniest creature that crawls at his feet, and refrains from killing or causing injury to any living being.

There is no rule that one is to be preyed upon by another. However, the strong do mercilessly kill the weak and feast on their flesh. This is animal instinct. Such actions by animals are excusable because they know not what they do, but when those who are gifted with reason and understanding perpetrate such crimes, there is no excuse. Whether to satisfy one's palate or as pastime, it is not justifiable to kill or to cause another living being to be killed. If the killing of animals is wrong, how much more heinous is it to kill human being individually or collectively employing brutal or so-called civilized methods for the sake of peace, religion, or any other seemingly good purpose?

Honesty, trustworthiness, and uprightness also are the

27

characteristics of a person with right understanding. Such a person tries to abstain from all forms of stealing "whether in its dissembled or obvious forms". Abstaining from sexual misconduct which debases the exalted nature of man, he tries to be pure and chaste. He avoids false speech, harsh language, slander and frivolous talks and speaks only what is true, sweet, kind and helpful. As certain drinks and drugs promote heedlessness and mental distraction, he avoids intoxicating liquor and cultivates heedfulness and clarity of vision.

These elementary principles of regulated behaviour are essential to one who treads the Path to *Nibbana* chiefly because they tend to control both deeds and words. Violation of them introduces obstacles that hinder his moral progress of the Path. Observance of them means smooth and steady progress along the Path.

Having progressed a step further in his gradual advance, the aspirant now tries to control his senses.

To control craving for food and to promote buoyancy of mind and body, abstemiousness or fasting at least once a month is advisable plain and simple living is preferable to a luxurious one which makes one a slave to passions. A life of celibacy is recommended, as one's valuable energy thus conserved could then be utilised wholly for the intellectual and moral welfare of oneself and others. In such a life, one is detached from additional worldly bond that impede moral progress. Almost all spiritual teachers, it would appear, have nourished their bodies sparingly and have led a life of strict celibacy, simplicity, voluntary poverty and self-control.

While he progresses slowly and steadily, with regulated words and deeds and sense-restraint, the Kammic force of the striving aspirant compels him to renounce worldly pleasures and adpot the ascetic life. To him·then comes the ideas that:

> "A dent or strife is household life,
>   And filled with toil and need,
>   But free and high as the open sky,
>   Is the life the homeless lead."

Thus realizing the vanity of sensual pleasures, he voluntarily forsakes all earthly possessions, and donning the ascetic garb tries to lead the Holy Life in all its purity.

MORE LAYMAN CAN REALIZE NIBBANA

It is not, however, the external appearance that makes a man holy but internal purification and an exemplary life. Transformation should come from within, not from without. It is absolutely necessary to retire to solitude and lead the life of an ascetic to realize *Nibbana*. The life of a Bhikkhu no doubt expedites and facilitates spiritual progress, but even as a laymen, Sainthood may be attained.

He who attains Arahatship (Sainthood) as a layman in the face of all temptations is certainly more praiseworthy than a Bhikkhu who attains Arahatship living admist surrounding that are not distracting.

Concerning a minister who attained Arahatship while seated on an elephant decked in his best apparel, the Buddha remarked:

> "Even though a man be richly adorned, if he walks in Peace

If he be quiet, subdued, certain and pure,
And if he refrains from injuring any living being,
That man is a Brahmin, that man is a hermit, that
man is a monk.[1]'

There have been several such instances of laymen who realized *Nibbana* without renouncing the world. The most devout and generous lay-follower Anathapindika was a *Sotapanna*[2], the Sakya Mahanama was a *Sakadagami*[3], the potter Ghatikara was an *Anagami*[4], and King Suddhodana died as an *Arahat*[5].

A BHIKKHU

A Bhikkhu is expected to observe the four kinds of Higher Morality – namely,

Patimokkha Sila – The Fundamental Moral Code[6].

Indriyasanvara Sila – Morality pertaining to sense-restraint.

Ajivaparisuddhi Sila – Morality pertaining to purity of livelihood.

Paccayasannissita Sila – Morality pertaining to the use of the necessaries of life.

---

1. *Dhammapada*, v. 142.
2. "Stream-Winner" – The first stage of Sainthood.
3. "Once-Returner" – The second stage of Sainthood.
4. "Never-Returner" – The third stage of Sainthood.
5. "The Worthy One" – The final stage of Sainthood.
6. Various rules which a Bhikkhu is expected to observe.

These four kinds of morality are collectively called *Sila-Visuddhi* (Purity of Virtue), the first of the seven stages of Purity on the way to *Nibbana.*

When a person enters the Orders and received his Higher (Upasampada) Ordination, he is called a Bhikkhu. There is no English equivalent that exactly conveys the meaning of this Pali term, "Bhikkhu". "Mendicant Monk" may be suggested as the nearest translation, not in the sense of one who begs but in the sense of one who lives on alms.

There are no vows for a Bhikkhu. Of his own accord, he becomes a Bhikkhu in order to lead the Holy Life as long as he likes. He is at liberty to leave the Order at any time.

A Bhikkhu is bound to observe 220 rules[1], apart from several other minor ones. The four major rules which deal with perfect celibacy, stealing, murder, and false claims to higher spiritual powers, must strictly be observed. If he violates any of them, he becomes defected (parajika) and automatically ceases to be a Bhikkhu. If he wishes, he can re-enter the Order and remain as a Samanera (novice). In the case of other rules, which he violates, he has to make amends according to the gravity of the offence.

Among the salient characteristics of a Bhikkhu are purity, perfect celibacy, voluntary poverty, humility, simplicity, selfless service, self-control, patience, compassion and harmlessness.

---

1. Excluding the seven modes of settling disputes *(adhikaranasmatha dhamma).*

The life of a Bhikkhu or, in other words, renunciation of worldly pleasures and ambitions is only an effective means to attain Nibbana, but is not an end in itself.

THE WAY TO NIBBANA (II)

MEDITATION

"One way to acquire gain, another that leads to *Nibbana*."

Dhammapada

CONCENTRATION (SAMADHI)

Securing a firm footing on the ground of morality, the aspirant then embarks upon the higher practice of *Samadhi,* the control and culture of mind, the second stage of the Path of Purity.

Samadhi is one-pointedness of the mind. It is concentration of the mind on one object to the entire exclusion of all else.

SUBJECTS OF MEDITATION

According to Buddhism there are forty subjects of meditation (kammatthana) which differ according to the temperaments of individuals.

They are:—

(a) The ten *Kasinas*[1] (devices)— namely:—

i. earth *Kasina,* ii. water *Kasina,* iii. fire *Kasina,* iv. air *Kasina,* v. blue *Kasina,* vi. yellow *Kasina,* vii. red *Kasina,* viii. white *Kasina,* ix. light *Kasina* and x. space *Kasina.*

33

(b) The ten Impurities (asubha)[2] — namely, ten corpses which are respectively:—

i. bloated (uddhumataka), ii. discoloured (vinila-ka), iii. festering (vipubbaka), iv. dissected (vic-chiddaka), v. gnawed-to-pieces (vikkhayitaka), vi. scattered-in-pieces (vikkhittaka), vii. mutilated and scattered-in-pieces (hata vikkhittaka),

---

1. *Kasina* here means whole, all complete. It is so called because the projected light issuing from the conceptualized image of the *Kasina* object could be extended everywhere without limitation.

In the case of earth *Kasina,* one makes a circle of about one span and four fingers in diameter and, covering it with dawn-coloured clay, smoothes it well. If there be not enough clay of the dawn colour, he may introduce some other kind of clay beneath. This concentrative circle is known as *Kasina-Mandala.* The remaining Kasinas should be similarly under-stood. Details are given in the *Visuddhi Magga.* It may be mentioned that light and space Kasinas are not found in the Text. When they are excluded, there are thirty-eight subjects.

2. These ten kinds of corpses were found in ancient cemeteries and charnel places where dead bodies were not buried or cremated and where flesh-eating beast and birds frequent. In modern days it is impossible to obtain such corpses as subject for meditation.

viii. bloody (lohitaka), ix. worm-infested (pulavaka), and x. skeleton (atthika).

(c) The ten Reflections (anussati)[1] — namely, eight Reflections on i. The Buddha (Buddhanussati), ii. The Doctrine (Dhammanussati), iii. The Sangha (Sanghanussati), vi. Virtue (silanussati), v. Liberality (caganussati), vi. Devas (devatanussati), vii. Peace (upasamanussati), viii. Death (maran-nusatti) respectively, together with ix. Mindfulness regarding the body (kayagatasati) and x.

(d) The four Illimitables or the Four Modes of Sublime Conduct (Brahmavihara) — namely, Loving-kindness (metta), Compassion (karuna), Sympathetic Joy (mudita), and Quanimity (upekkha).

(e) The One Perception — i.e., the Perception of the loathsomeness of material food (ahare patikkulasanna)[2].

(f) The One Analysis — i.e., The Analysis of the four Elements (catudhatuvavatthana)[3].

---

1. *Anussati* — lit. means constant mindfulness. Mindfulness regarding respiration (anapanasati).

2. *Ahare patikkulasanna* — i.e., the feeling of loathsomeness of good in its search, eating etc.

3. *Catudhatuvavatthana* — i.e., the investigation of the four primary elements of extension (pathavi), cohesion (apo), heat (tejo) and motion (vayo) will regard to their special characteristics.

(g)   The four Arupa Jhanas — namely,

The Realm of the Infinity of Space (Akasanan-cayatana), The Realm of the Infinity of Conscious-ness (Vinnanancayatana), The Realm of Nothing-ness (Akincannayatana), and the Realms of neither Perception nor non-Perception (Neva sanna nasan-nayatana).

SUITABILITY OF SUBJECTS FOR DIFFERENT TEMPE-RAMENTS

According to the Texts, the ten Impurities and the Mindfulness regarding the Body such as the thirty-two parts are suitable for those of a lustful temperament because they tend to create a disgust for the body which fascinates the sense.

The four Illimitables and the four coloured *Kasinas* are suitable for those of a hateful temperament.

The Reflections of the Buddha and so forth are suitable for those of a devout temperament. The Reflection on Death and Peace, Perception on the loathsomeness of material food, and Analysis of the four Elements are suitable for those of an intellectual temperament. The remaining objects, chiefly the Reflection on the Buddha, Meditation on Loving-Kindness, Mindfulness regarding the Body and Reflection on Death are suitable for all, irrespective of temperament.

SIX KINDS OF TEMPERAMENTS

There are six kinds of Temperaments (carita) They are—

i. Lustful Temperament (ragacarita),
ii. Hateful Temperament (dosacarita),
iii. Ignorant Temperament (mohacarita),
iv. Devout Temperament (saddhacarita),
v. Intellectual Temperament (buddhicarita), and
vi. Discursive Temperament (vitakkacarita).

Charita signifies the intrinsic nature of a person which is revealed when one is in normal state without being preoccupied with anything. The temperaments of people differ owing to the diversity of their actions or *Kamma*. Habitual actions tend to form particular temperaments.

Raga or lust is predominant in some, while *dosa* or anger, hatred, illwill in others. Most people belong to these two categories. There are a few others who lack intelligence and are more or less ignorant (mohacarita). Akin to ignorant are those whose minds ocillate unable to focus their attention deliberately on one thing (vitakkacarita). By nature some are exceptionally devout, while others are exceptionally intelligent (buddhicarita).

Combining these six with one another, we get 63 types. With the inclusion of speculative Temperament (ditticarita), there are 64 types.

The subjects of meditation are variously adapted to these different temperaments and types of people.

PRACTICE OF CONCENTRATION

Before practising *Samadhi*, the qualified aspirant should give a careful consideration to the subject of meditation. In ancient days, it was cutomary for pupils to seek the guidance of a competent teacher to choose a suitable subject according to their temperaments. But, today if no competent teacher is available, the aspirant must exercise his own judgement and choose one he thinks most suited to his character.

When the subject has been chosen, he should withdraw to a quiet place where there are the fewest distractions. The forest, a cave, or any lonely place is most desirable, for there one is least liable to interruption during the practice.

It should be understood that solitude is within us all. If our minds are not settled, even a quiet forest would not be a congenial place. If our minds are settled, even the heart of a busy town may be congenial. The atmosphere in which we live acts as an indirect aid to tranquillize our minds.

Next to be decided by the aspirant in the most convenient time when he himself and his surrounding are in the best possible condition for the practice.

Early in the morning when the mind is fresh and active, or before bedtime, if one is not overtired, is generally the most appropriate time for meditation. But whatever the time selected, it is advisable daily to keep to that particular hour, for our minds then become conditioned to the practice.

The meditating posture, too serves as a powerful method for concentration.

Easterners generally sit cross-legged, with the body erect. They sit placing the right foot on the left thigh and the left foot on the right thigh. This is the full position. If this posture is difficult, as it certainly is to many, the half position may be adopted, that is, simply placing the right foot on the left thigh or the left on the right thigh.

When this triangular position is assumed, the whole body is well balanced.

The right hand should be placed on the left hand, the neck straightened so that the nose is in a perpendicular line with the navel. The tongue should rest on the upper palate. The belt should be loosened, and clothes neatly adjusted. Some prefer closed eyes so as to shut out all unnecessary light and external sights.

Although there are certain advantages in closing the eyes, it is not always recommended as it tends to drowsiness. Then the mind gets out of control and wanders aimlessly, vagrant thoughts arise, the body loses its erectness, quite unconsciously the mouth opens itself, saliva drivels, and the head nods.

The Buddhas usually sit with half closed eyes looking through the tip of the nose not more than a distance of four feet away.

Those who find the cross-legged posture too difficult may sit comfortably in a chair or any other support, sufficiently high to rest the feet on the ground.

It is of no great importance what attitude one adopts provided the position is easy and relaxed.

HOW TO SUBDUE EVIL THOUGHTS

The aspirant who is striving to gain one-pointedness of the mind should endeavour to control any unwholesome thoughts at their very inception.

As mentioned in the *Sutta Nipata*, he may be attacked by the ten armies of the Evil One. They are: i. sensual desires (kama), ii. discouragement (arati), iii. hunger and thirst (khuppipasa), iv. attachment (tanha), v. sloth and torpor (thinamiddha), vi. fear (bhaya), vii. doubt (vicikiccha), viii. detraction and stubborness (makkha, thambha), ix. ill-gotten gain, praise, honour and fame (labha, siloka, sakkara, micchayasa), and x. self-praise and contempt for others (attukkamsana paravambhana).

On such occasions, the following practical suggestions given by the Buddha will be beneficial to all:—

1. Harbouring a good thought opposite to the en-croaching one, e.g. loving-kindness in case of hatred.

2. Reflecting upon possible evil consequences, e.g. anger sometimes results in murder.

3. Simple neglect or becoming wholly inattentive to them.

4. Tracing the cause which led to the arising of the unwholesome thoughts and thus forgetting them in the retrospective process.

5. Direct physical force.

Just as a strong man overpowers a weak person, so one

should overcome evil thoughts by bodily strength. "With teeth clenched and tongue pressed to the palate," advises the Buddha, "the monk by main force must constrain and coerce his mind and thus with clenched teeth and taut tongue, constraining and coercing his mind, those evil and unsalutary thoughts will disappear and go to decay; and with their disappearing, the mind will become settled, subdued, unified and concentrated."

Having attended to all these necessary preliminaries, the qualified aspirant retires to a solitary place, and summoning up confidence as to the certainty of achieving his goal, he makes a persistent effort to develop concentration.

A physical object like a *Kasina* circle only aids concentration. But a virtue like loving-kindness has the specific advantage of building up that particular virtue in the character of the person.

While meditating, one may intelligently repeat the words of special formula, since they serve as an aid to evoke the ideas they represent.

However intent the aspirant may be on the object of his meditation he will not be exempted from the initial difficulties that inevitably confront a beginner. "The mind wanders, alien thoughts dance before him, impatience overcomes him owing to the slowness of progress, and his efforts slacken in consequence." The determined aspirant only welcomes these obstacles, the difficulties he cuts through and looks straight to his goal, never for a moment turning away his eyes from it.

CONCENTRATION ON EARTH – KASINA

Suppose, for instance, an aspirant takes an earth-*kasina* for his object (kammatthana).

The surface of a circle of about one foot in diameter is covered with clay and smoothed well. This concentrative circle is known as the preliminary object (parikamma nimitta). He sets it down some four feet away and concentrates on it, saying *pathavi pathavi,* (earth, earth) until he becomes so wholly absorbed in it that all adventitious thoughts get automatically excluded from the mind. When he does this for some time – perhaps weeks or months or years – he would be able to visualize the object with closed eyes. On this visualized image (uggaha nimitta), which is a mental replica of the object, he concentrates until it develops into a conceptualized image (patibhaga nimitta).

According to the *Visuddhi Magga*, the difference between the first visualized image and the second conceptualized image is that "in the former, a fault of the *kasina* object appears while the latter is like the disc of a mirror taken out of a bag, or a well-burnished conch shell, or the round moon issuing from the clouds."

The conceptualized image neither possesses colour nor form. It is just a mode of appearance and is born of perception.

As he continually concentrates on this abstract concept, he is said to be in possession of "proximate concentration (upacara samadhi) and the innate five Hindrances to spiritual progress (nivarana) namely, sensual desires (kamacchanda), hatred (vyapada), sloth and torper (thinamiddha), restlessness and worry (uddhacca kukkucca) and indecision (vicikiccha), are temporarily inhibited by means of one-pointedness (ekaggata), zest (piti), initial application (vitakka), happiness (sukha) and sustained application (vicara) respectively.

Eventually he gains 'ecstatic concentration' (appana samadhi) and becomes absorbed in *Jhana,* enjoying the calmness and serenity of a one-pointed mind.

This one-pointedness of the mind, achieved by inhibiting the Hindrances, is termed 'Purity of Mind' (cittavisuddhi), the second stage on the Path of Purity.

For the water-*kasina* one may take a vessel full of colourless water, preferably rain water, and concentrate on it, saying — apo, apo, (water, water) until he gains one-pointedness of the mind.

To develop the fire-*kasina* one may kindle a fire before him and concentrate on it through a hole, a span and four fingers wide, in a rush-mat, a piece of leather, or a piece of cloth.

One who develops the air-*kasina* concentrate on the wind that enters through a window-space or a hole in the wall, saying — vayo, vayo, (air, air).

To develop the colour-kasinas, one may make a disc (mandala) of the prescribed size and colour of blue, yellow, red, or white and concentrate on it, repeating name of the colour as in the case of the earth-*kasina.*

He may even concentrate on blue, yellow, red and white flowers.

43

Light-*kasina* may be developed by concentrating on the moon or an unflickering lamplight or on a circle of light made on the ground or the wall by sunlight or moonlight entering through a wall-crevice or holes saying — aloka, aloka (light, light).

Space-*kasina* could be developed by concentrating on a hole, a span and four fingers wide, in either a well-covered pavilion or a piece of leather or a mat saying — okasa, okasa (space, space).

ASUBHA

The ten kinds of corpses were found in ancient Indian cemeteries where dead bodies were not buried or cremated and flesh-eating animals frequent. In modern days, finding them is out of question.

ANUSSATI

Buddhanussati — is the reflection on the virtues of the Buddha as follows: —

"Such indeed is that Exalted One — Worthy, Fully Enlightened, Endowed with Wisdom and Conduct, Well-farer, Knower of the Worlds, an Incomparable Charioteer for the Training of individuals. Teacher of gods and men, Omniscient and Holy."

Dhammanussati — is the reflection on the virtues of the characteristics of the Doctrine as follows: —

"Well-expounded is the doctrine by the Blessed One, to be realized by oneself of immediate fruits inviting investigation, leading to Nibbana to be understood by the wise, each one for himself."

Sanghanussati — is the reflection on the virtues of the pure members of the Holy Celibate Order as follows:-

"Of good conduct is the Order of the disciples of the Blessed One; upright conduct is the Order of the disciples of the Blessed One; of wise conduct is the Order of the disciples of the Blessed One; of dutiful conduct is the Order of the disciples of the Blessed One. These four pairs of person constitute eight individuals. This Order or the disciples of the Blessed One is worthy of offerings, is worthy of hospitality, is worthy of gifts, is worthy of reverential salutation, is an incomparable field of merit to the world.

Silanussati — is the reflection on the perfection of one's own virtuous conduct.

Caganussati — is the reflection on one's own charitable nature.

Devatanussati — "Deities are born in such exalted states on account of their faith and other virtues, I too possess them." Thus when one reflects again and again on one's own faith and other virtues, placing deities as witnesses, it is called *Devatanussati.*

Upasamanussati — is the reflection on the attributes of *Nibbana* such as the cessation of suffering and the like.

Marananussati — is the reflection on the termination of

Psycho-Physical.

Contemplation on death enables one to comprehend the fleeting nature of life. When one understands that death is certain and life is uncertain; one endeavours to make the best use of one's life by working for self-development and for the development of others instead of wholly indulging in sensual pleasures. Constant meditation on death does not make one pessimistic and lethargic, but, on the contrary, it makes one more active and energetic. Besides, one can face death with serenity.

While contemplating death, one may think that life is like a flame or that all so-called beings are the outward temporary manifestations of the invisible Kammic energy just as an electric light is the outward manifestation of the invisible electric energy. Use various similes as one likes, one may meditate on the uncertainty of life and on the certainty of death.

Kayagatasati – is the reflection on the 32 impure parts of the body such as hair, hair of the body, nails, teeth, skin, flesh, sinews, bones, marrow, kidneys, heart, liver, diaphragm, spleen, lungs, bowels, mesentery, stomach, faeces, brain, bile, phelgm, pus, blood, sweat, lymph, tears, grease, saliva, nasal mucus, articular fluid and urine.

This meditation on the loathsomeness of the body leads to dispassion. Many Bhikkhus in the time of the Buddha attained Arahatship by meditating on these impurities. If one is not conversant with all the thirty-two parts, one may meditate on one part such as bones, flesh, or skin.

Inside this body is found a skeleton. It is filled with

flesh which is covered with a skin. Beauty is nothing but skin deep. When one reflects on the impure parts of the body in this manner, passionate attachment to this body gradually disappears.

This meditation may not appeal to those who are not sensual. They may meditate on the innate creative possibilities of this complex machinery of man.

ANAPANASATI

Anapanasati — is mindfulness on respiration. *Ana* means exhalation and *apana,* inhalation.

Concentration on the breathing process leads to one-pointedness of the mind and ultimately to Insight which leads to Arahatship.

This is one of the best subjects of meditation which appeals equally to all. The Buddha also practised this *anapanasati* before His Enlightenment. A detailed exposition of this meditation is found in the *Satipatthana Sutta* and in the *Visuddhi Magga.*

A few practical hints are given here for the benefit of the average reader.

Adopting a convenient posture, breathe out and close the mouth. Then breathe through the nostrils naturally and not forcefully. Inhale first and mentally count one. Exhale and count two, concentrating on the breathing process. In this manner, one may count up to ten constantly focussing one's attention on respiration. It is possible for the mind to

47

wander before one counts up to ten. But one need not be discouraged. Let one try till one succeeds. Gradually one may increase the number of series — say five series of ten. Later one may concentrate on respiration without counting. Some prefer counting as it aids concentration, while some others prefer not to count. What is essential is concentration and not counting which is secondary. When one does this concentration, one feels light in body and mind and very peaceful too. One might perhaps feel as if one were floating in the air. When this concentration is practised for a certain period, a day will come when one will realize that so-called body is supported by mere breath and that body perishes when breathing ceases. One instantly realizes impermanence. Where there is change there cannot be a permanent entity or an immortal soul. Insight could then be developed to gain Arahatship.

It is now clear that the object of this concentration on respiration is not merely to gain one-pointedness but also to cultivate Insight in order to obtain deliverance.

This simple method may be pursued by all without any harm.

For more details, readers are to refer to the *Visuddhi Magga. Anapanasati* according to the *Satipatthana Sutta:—*

"Mindfully he inhales, mindfully he exhales."

1.   "When making a long inhalation, he knows: 'I make a long inhalation'; when making a long exhalation, he knows: 'I make a long exhalation'."

2.   "When making a short inhalation, he knows: 'I make a

short inhalation'; when making a short exhalation, he knows: 'I make a short exhalation'."

3. "Clearly perceiving the entire breathing process, (i.e., the beginning, middle and end), I will inhale': thus he trains himself; 'clearly perceiving the entire breathing process, I will exhale'; thus he trains himself."

4. "Calming the respirations, I will inhale': thus he trains himself; 'calming the respirations, I will exhale'; thus he trains himself."

ABHINNA

When once the aspirant succeeds in cultivating the jhanas, he can without difficulty, develop the five supernormal powers (abhinna) — namely, Divine Eye (dibbacakhu), Divine Ear (dibbasota), Reminiscence of past births (pubbe-nivasanussatinana), Thought-reading (paracittavijanana), and various psychic powers (iddhividha).

Samadhi and these supernormal powers, it may be mentioned, are not essential for the attainment of Arahatship, though they would undoubtedly be an asset to the possessor. There are, for instance, dry-visioned Arahats (sukkhavipassaka) who, without the aid of the jhanas, attain Arahatship straightaway by merely cultivating Insight. Many men and women attained Arahatship in the time of the Buddha Himself without developing the jhanas.

It is only one who has gained the fifth *jhana* that could develop the five kinds of *Abhinna.*

Dibbacakkhu is the Celestial or Divine Eye, also called clairvoyance, which enables one to see heavenly or earthly things, far or near, that are imperceptible to the physical eye.

Cutupapatanana, knowledge with regard to the dying and reappearing of beings, is identical with this Celestial Eye. Knowledge with regard to the future and knowledge with regard to the faring of beings according to their own good and bad actions, are two other kinds of Knowledge belonging to the same category.

Dibbasota is the Celestial Ear, also called clairaudience, which enables one to hear subtle or coarse sounds far or near.

Pubbenivasanussatinana is the power to remember the past lives of oneself and others. With regard to this knowledge, the Buddha's power is limitless, while in the case of others it is limited.

Iddhividha is the power to fly through the air, walk on water, dive into the earth, create new forms, etc.

NIVARANA OR HINDRANCES

"There are these five corruptions of the heart, tainted by which the heart is neither soft, not pliable, nor gleaming, nor easily broken up, nor perfectly composed for the destruction of the corruptions."

Samyutta Nikaya

Nivarana ((Nivar) to hinder, to obstruct) is that which hinders one's progress or that which obstructs the path to

Emancipation and heavenly states. It is also explained as that which "muffles, enwraps, or trammels thought."

There are five kinds of Nivaranas or Hindrances. They are: (1) Sensual desires (Kamacchanda). (2) Illwill (Vyapada), (3) Sloth and Torpor (Thina-Middha), (4) Restlessness and Worry (Uddhacca-Kukkucca), and (5) Doubts (Vicikiccha).

1.   *Kamacchanda* means sensual desires or attachment to pleasure sense-objects such as form, sound, odour, taste, and contact. This is regarded as one of the Fetters, too, that bind one to *Samsara.*

An average person is bound to get tempted by these alluring objects of sense. Lack of self-control results in the inevitable arising of passions. This Hindrance is inhibited by One-pointedness (Ekaggata), which is one of the five characteristics of *Jhanas.* It is attenuated on attaining *Sakadagami* and is completely eradicated on attaining *Anagami.* Subtle forms of attachment such as *Rupa Raga* and *Arupa Raga* (Attachment to Realms of Form and Formless Realms) are eradicated only on attaining Arahatship.

The following six conditions tend to the eradication of sense-desires: (i) perceiving the loathsomeness of the object, (ii) constant meditation on loathsomeness, (iii) sense-restraint, (iv) moderation in food, (v) good friendship, and (vi) profitable talk.

2.   *Vyapada* is illwill or aversion. A desirable object leads to attachment while an undesirable one leads to aversion. These are the two great fires that burn the whole world. Aided by ignorance these two produce all sufferings

in the world.

Illwill in inhibited by Pity or joy which is one of the *Jhana* factors. It is attenuated on attaining *Sakadagami* and is eradicated on attaining *Anagami.*

The following are six conditions which tend to the eradication of illwill: (i) perceiving the object with thoughts of goodwill, (ii) constant meditation on loving-kindness (Metta), (iii) thinking that *Kamma* is one's own, (iv) adherence to that view, (v) good friendship, and (vi) profitable talk.

3. *Thina* or sloth is explained as a morbid state of the mind, and *Middha* as a morbid state of the mental states. A stolid mind is as inert as a bat hanging to a tree, or as molasses cleaving to a stick, or as a lump of butter too stiff for spreading." Sloth and torpor should not be understood as bodily drowsiness, because Arahats, who have destroyed these two states, also experience bodily fatigue. These two promote mental inertness and are opposed to strenuous effort (Viriya). They are inhibited by the *Jhana* factor *Vitakka* or Initial Application, and are eradicated on attaining Arahatship.

The following six conditions tend to the eradication of Sloth and Torpor: (i) reflection on the object of moderation of food, (ii) changing of bodily postures, (iii) comtemplation on the object of light, (iv) living in the open, (v) good friendship and (vi) profitable talk.

4. *Uddhacca* is mental restlessness or excitement of the mind. It is a mental state associated with all types of immoral consciousness. As a rule an evil is done with some

excitement or restlessness.

Kukkucca is worry. It is either repentance over the committed evil or over the unfulfilled good. Repentance over one's evil does not exempt one from its evitable consequences. The best repentance is the will not to repeat that evil.

Both these hindrances are inhibited by the *Jhana* factor, *Sukha* or happiness. Restlessness is eradicated on attaining Arahatship, and worry is eradicated on attaining *Anagami.*

The following six conditions tend to the eradication of these two states: (i) erudition or learning, (ii) questioning or discussion, (iii) understanding the nature of the Vinaya discipline, (iv) association with senior monks, (v) good friendship and (vi) profitable talk.

5. *Vicikkiccha* is doubt or indecision. That which is devoid of the remedy of wisdom is *vicikkiccha* (vi = devoid; cikiccha = wisdom). It is also explained as vexation due to perplexed thinking (vici = seeking; kiccha = vexation).

Here it is not used in the sense of doubt with regard to the Buddha etc., for even non-Buddhists inhibit *vicikiccha* and gain *Jhanas.* As a Fetter, *vicikiccha* is that doubt about Buddha, etc. But as a Hindrance, it denotes unsteadiness in one particular thing that is being done. The commentarial explanation of *vicikiccha* is the inability to decide anything definitely that it is so. In other words, it is indecision.

This state is inhibited by the *Jhana* factor — *Vicara*, Sustained Application. It is eradicated on attaining *Sotapatti.*

The following six conditions tend to its eradication: (i) knowledge of the Dhamma and Vinaya, (ii) discussion or questioning, (iii) understanding of the nature of the Vinaya Discipline, (iv) excessive confidence, (v) good friendship, and (vi) profitable talk.

THE WAY TO NIBBANA (III)

"Transient are all component things,
Sorrowful are all component things,
Soulless are all conditioned and non-conditioned.

Dhammapada

INSIGHT (VIPASSANA)

When the Jhanas are developed by temporarily inhibiting the Hindrances (Nivarana), the mind is so purified that it resembles a polished mirror, where everything is clearly reflected in true perspective. Still there is not complete freedom from unwholesome thoughts, for by concentration, the evil tendencies are only temporarily inhibited. They may rise to the surface at quite unexpected moments.

Discipline regulates words and deeds: concentration controls the mind; but it is Insight (panna), the third and final stage, that enables the aspirant to Sainthood to eradicate wholly the defilements inhibited by *Samadhi.*

At the outset, he cultivates 'Purity of Vision' (ditthi visuddhi) in order to see things as they truly are. With one-pointed mind, he analyses and examines this so-called being. This searching examination shows what he has called "I" personality, to be merely a complex compound of mind and matter which are in a state of constant flux.

Having thus gained a correct view of the real nature of this so-called being, freed from the false notion of a permanent soul, he searches for the causes of this "I" personality. He realizes that there is nothing in the world but is conditioned by some cause or causes, past or present, and that his present existence is due to past ignorance (avijja), craving (tanha), grasping (upadana), *Kamma* and physical food of the present life. On account of these five causes, this so-called being has arisen, and as past causes have conditioned the present, so the present will condition the future. Meditating thus, he transcend all doubts with regards to past, present and future.

Thereupon he contemplates the truth that all conditioned things are transients (anicca), subject to suffering (dukkha), and devoid of an immortal soul (anatta). Whenever he turns his eyes, he sees naught but these three characteristics standing out in bold relief. He realizes that life is a more flux conditioned by internal cause. Nowhere does he find any genuine happiness, for everything is fleeting.

As he thus contemplates the real nature of life and is absorbed in meditation, a day comes when, to his surprise, he witnesses an aura (obhasa) emitted by his body. He experiences an unprecedented pleasure, happiness and quietude. He becomes even-minded, religious fervour increases, mindfulness becomes clear and insight keen, mistaking this advanced state of moral progress for Sainthood, chiefly owing to the presence of the aura, he develops a liking to this mental state. Soon the realization comes that these new developments are impediments to moral progress and he cultivates the purity of knowledge with regard to the Path and Not-Path.

Perceiving the right path, he resumes his meditation in the arising (udaya nana) and passing away (vaya nana) of all conditioned things. Of these two states, the later becomes more impressed on his mind since change is more conspicious than becoming. Therefore, he directs his attention to contemplation of the dissolution of things (bhanga nana). He perceives that both mind and matter which constitute this so-called being are in a state of constant flux, not remaining for two consecutive moments the same. To him then comes the knowledge that all dissolving things are fearful (bhaya nana). The whole world appears to him as a pit of burning embers — a source of danger. Subsequently he reflects on the wretchedness and vanity (adinava nana) of the fearful and deluded world, and gets a feeling of disgust (nibbida nana) followed by a strong will for deliverance from it (muncitu-kamyata nana).

With this object in view, he resumes his meditations on the three characteristics of transiency, sorrow, and soulless-ness (patisankha nana) and thereafter develops complete equanimity towards all conditioned things having neither attachment nor aversion for any worldly object (upekkha nana).

Reaching this point of spiritual, he chooses one of the three, cultivates insight in that particular direction until the glorious characteristic for his object of special endeavour and intently day when he first realizes *Nibbana,* his ultimate goal.

"As the traveller by night sees the landscape around him by a flash of lighting and the picture so obtained, swims long there after before his dazzled eyes, so the individual seekers, by the flashing light of insight, glimpses *Nibbana* with such clearness that the after-picture never more fades from his mind."

When the spiritual pilgrim realizes *Nibbana* for the first time, he is called a *Sotapanna,* one who has entered the stream that leads to *Nibbana* for the first time.

The Stream represents the Noble Eightfold Path.

A Stream-Winner is no more a worldling (puthujjana), but an *Ariya* (Noble)

1. These nine kinds of insight — namely *udaya, vaya, bhanga, bhaya, adinava, nibbida, muncitukamyata, patisamkha,* and *upekkha nanas* are collectively termed *Patipadananadassanavisuddhi* — of Purity of Vision as Path of Purity.

2. Insight found in this supramundane Path Consciousness is known as *Nanadassana vissuddhi* — Purity of Vision which is knowledge, the seventh member of the Path of Purity.

FETTERS — SAMYOJANA

On attaining this first stage of Sainthood, he eradicates the following three Fetters (samyojana) that bind him to existence — namely,

i. *Sakkaya-ditthi* = *sati kaye ditthi* — literally, view when a group or compound exists. Here *kaya* refers to the five Aggregates of matter, feeling, perception, mental state, and consciousness. The view that there exists an unchanging entity, a permanent soul, when there is a complex compound of psycho-physical aggregates is termed *sakkaya-ditthi. Dhammasangani* enumerates twenty kinds of such soul-theories. *Sakkaya-ditthi* is usually rendered as self-illusion, theory of individuality, or illusion of individualism.

ii.   *Vicikicca* – Doubts. They are doubts about (i) the Buddha, (ii) the Dhamma, (iii) the Sangha, (iv) the disciplinary rules (sikkha), (v) the past, (vi) the future, (vii) both the past and the future, and (viii) Dependent Origination (Paticca-Samuppada).

iii.   *Silabbataparamasa* – Adherence to (wrongful) rites and ceremonies.

Dhammasangani explains it thus: "It is the theory held by ascetics and Brahmins outside this doctrine that purification is obtained by rules of moral conduct and rites."

SOTAPANNA – STREAM-WINNER

For the eradication of the remaining seven Fetters, a Sotapanna is reborn seven times at the most. He gains implicit confidence in the Buddha, the Dhamma and the Sangha. He would not for any reason violate any of the five precepts. He is not subjected to rebirth in states of woe as he is destined to Enlightenment.

With fresh courage as a result of these distant glimpse of *Nibbana,* the noble pilgrim makes a rapid progress, and perfecting his insight becomes a *Sakadagami* (Once-Returner), the second stage of Sainthood, by attenuating two other Fetters – namely, sense-desires (kamaraga) and illwill (patigha).

Now he is called a Once-Returner because he is born in the human realm only once, should he not attain Arahatship in that birth itself. It is interesting to note that the *Ariya* Saint who has attained the second stage of Sainthood can only weaken these two powerful Fetters with which he is bound from a beginningless past. At times, though to a slight extent, he may harbour thoughts of lust and anger.

It is by attaining the third stage of Sainthood, that of the *Anagami* (Never-Returner), that he completely eradicates those two Fetters. Thereafter he neither returns to this world nor is he born in the celestial realms, since he has rooted out the desire for sensual gratification. After death, he is reborn in the Pure Abodes (Suddhavasa), an environment reserved for Anagamis. There he attains Arahatship and lives till the end of his life.

When a layman becomes an *Anagami,* he leads a celibate life.

The *Anagami* Saint now makes his final advance and destroying the remaining five Fetters — namely, attachment to Realms of Form (ruparaga), attachment to Formless Realms (aruparaga), pride (mana), restlessness (uddhacca), and ignorance (avijja) — attains Arahatship, the final stage of Sainthood.

Stream-Winners, Once-Returners, Never-Returners are called *Sekhas* because they have yet to undergo a training. Arahats are called *Asekhas* (Adepts) because they no more undergo any training.

An *Arahat,* literally, A Worthy One, is not subjected to rebirth because he does not accumulate fresh Kammic activities. The seeds of his reproduction have all been destroyed.

60

ARAHAT – SAINT

The *Arahat* realizes that what was to be accomplished has been done, a heavy burden of sorrow has finally been relinquished, and all forms of craving and all shades of ignorance are totally annihilated. The happy pilgrim now stands on heights more than celestial, far removed from uncontrolled passions and the defilements of the world, experiencing the unutterable bliss of *Nibbana.*

Rebirth can no longer affect him since no more reproductive seeds are formed by fresh kammic activities.

Though an Arahat, he is not wholly free from physical suffering, as this experience of the bliss of Deliverance is only intermittent nor has he yet cast off his material body.

An *Arahat* is called an *Asekha,* one who does not undergo training, as he has lived the Holy Life and has accomplished his object. The other Saints from the Sotapatti stage to the Arahat Path Stage are called *Sekhas* because they still undergo training.

It may be mentioned in this connection that *Anagamis* and *Arahats* who have developed the *Rupa* and *Arupa Jhanas* could experience the Nibbanic bliss uninterruptedly for as long as seven days even in this life. This, in Pali, is known as *Nirodha-Samapatti.* An *Ariya,* in this stage, is wholly free from pain, and his mental activities are all suspended. His stream of consciousness temporarily ceases to flow.

With regard to the difference between one who has attained *Nirodha-Samapatti* and a dead man, the *Visuddhi*

Magga states: "In the corpse not only are the plastic forces of the body (i.e., respiration), speech and mind stilled and quiescent, but also vitality is exhausted, heat is quenched, and the faculties are clear, although respiration, observation, and perception are stilled and quiescent."

According to Buddhism, in conventional terms, this is the highest form of bliss possible in this life.

WHAT IS NIBBANA?

Nibbana is the summum bonum of Buddhism.

However clearly and descriptively one may write on this profound subject, however glowing may be the terms in which one attempts to describe its utter serenity, comprehension of *Nibbana* is impossible by mere perusal of books. *Nibbana* is not something to be set down in print, nor is it a subject to be grasped by intellect alone; it is a supramundane state (Lokuttara Dhamma) to be realized only by intuitive wisdom.

A purely intellectual comprehension of *Nibbana* is impossible because it is not a matter to be arrived at by logical reasoning. The words of the Buddha are perfectly logical, but *Nibbana,* the ultimate Goal of Buddhism, is beyond the scope of logic. Nevertheless, by reflecting on the positive and negative aspects of life, the logical conclusion emerges that in contradistinction to a conditioned phenomenal existence, there must exist a sorrowless, deathless, non-conditioned State.

The *Jataka* Commentary relates that the Bodhisatta himself in his birth as the ascetic Sumedha contemplated thus:—

> "Even as, although Misery is,
>   Yet Happiness is also found,
>   So, though indeed Existence is,
>   No-existence should be sought."

> "Even as, although there may be Heat,
>   Yet grateful Cold is also found,
>   So, though the threefold Fire exists,

63

Likewise Nibbana should be sought."

"Even as, although there Evil is,
That which is Good is also found,
So, though 'tis true that birth exists,
That which is not birth should be sought."

DEFINITION

The Pali word *Nibbana* (Sanskrit — *Nirvana)* is composed of 'Ni' and 'Vana'. Ni is a negative particle. *Vana* means weaving or craving. This craving serves as a cord to connect one life with another.

"It is called *Nibbana* in that it is a departure (Ni) from that craving which is called *Vana,* lusting."

As long as one is bound up by craving or attachment one accumulates fresh Kammic activities which must materialise in one form or other in the eternal cycle of birth and death. When all forms of craving are eradicated, reproductive Kammic forces cease to operate, and one attains *Nibbana,* escaping the cycle of birth and death. The Buddhist conception of Deliverance is escape from the ever-recurring cycle of life and death and not merely an escape from sin and hell.

Nibbana is also explained as the extinction of the fire of lust (lobha), hatred (dosa) and delusion (moha).

"The whole world is in flames." says the Buddha. "By what fire is it kindled? By the fire of lust, hatred and delusion; by the fire of birth, old age, death, sorrow lamentation, pain, grief and despair is it kindled."

Nibbana, in one sense, may be interpreted as the extinction of these flames. One must not thereby infer that *Nibbana* is nothing but the extinction of these flames. The means should be differentiated from the end. Here the extinction of the flames is the means of attaining *Nibbana.*

IS NIBBANA NOTHINGNESS?

To say that *Nibbana* is nothingness simply because one cannot perceive it with the five senses, is as illogical as to conclude that light does not exist simply because the blind do not see it. In a well-known fable, the fish, who was acquainted only with water, arguing with the turtle, triumphantly concluded that there existed no land, because he received "No" to all his queries.

"Once upon a time there was a fish. And just because it was a fish, it had lived all its life in the water and knew nothing whatever about anything else but water. And one day as it swam about in the pond where all its days had been spent, it happened to meet a turtle of its acquaintance who had just come back from a little excursion on the land."

"Good day, Mr. Turtle!" said the fish, "have not seen you for a long time. Where have you been?"

"Oh," said the turtle, "I have just been for a trip on dry land."

"On dry land!" exclaimed the fish. "What do you mean by on dry land? There is no dry land. I had never seen such a thing. Dry land is nothing."

"Well," said the turtle good-naturedly. "If you want to think so, of course you may, there is no one who can hinder you. But that's where I've been, all the same."

"O come," said the fish. "Try to talk sense. Just tell me now what is this land of yours like? Is it all wet?"

"No, it is not wet," said the turtle.

"Is it nice and fresh and cool?" asked the fish.

"No, it is not nice and fresh and cool," the turtle replied.
"Is it clear so that light can come through it?"

"No, it is not clear. Light cannot come through it."

"Is it soft and yielding, so that I could move my fins about it and push my nose through it?"

"No, it is not soft and yielding. You could not swim in it."

"Does it move or flow in streams?"

"No, it neither moves nor flows in streams."

"Does it ever rise up into waves then, with white foams in them?" asked the fish, impatient at this string of Noes.

"No!" replied the turtle truthfully, "It never rises up into waves that I have seen."

"There now," exclaimed the fish triumphantly. "Didn't

I tell you that this land of yours was just nothing? I have just asked, and you have answered me that it is neither wet nor cool, not clear, nor soft and that it does not flow in streams nor rise up into waves. And if it isn't a single one of these things what else is it but nothing? Don't tell me."

"Well, well," said the turtle. "If you are determined to think that dry land is nothing, I suppose you must just go on thinking so. But any one who knows what is water and what is land would say you were just a silly fish, for you think that anything you have never known is nothing just because you have never known it."

And with that the turtle turned away and leaving the fish behind in its little pond of water, set out on another excursion over the dry land that was nothing.

It is evident from this significant story that neither can the turtle, who is acquainted with both land and sea, explain to the fish the real nature of land, nor can the fish grasp what is land since it is acquainted only with the sea. In the same way, *Arahats* who are acquainted with both the mundane and the supramundane cannot explain to a worldling what exactly the supramundance is in mundance terms, nor can a worlding understand the supramundane merely by mundane knowledge.

If *Nibbana* is nothingness, then it necessarily must coincide with space (Akasa). Both space and *Nibbana* are eternal and unchanging. The former is eternal because it is nothing in itself. The latter is spaceless and *Nibbana*, it may briefly be said that space is not, but *Nibbana* is.

The Buddha speaking of the different planes of existence makes special reference to a 'Realm of Nothingness' (Akincannayatana).

The fact that *Nibbana* is realized as one of the mental objects decidedly proves that it is not a state of nothingness. If it were so, the Buddha would not have described its state in such terms as "Infinite" (Ananta), "Non-conditioned" (Asamkhata), "Incomparable" (Anupameya), "Supreme" (Anuttara), "Highest" (Para), "Beyond" (Para), "Highest Refuge" (Parayana), "Safety" (Tana), "Security" (Khema), "Happiness" (Siva), "Unique" (Kevala), "Abodeless" (Analaya), "Imperishable" (Akkhara), "Absolute Purity" (Visuddha), "Supramundane" (Lokuttara), "Immortality" (Amata), "Emancipation" (Mutti), "Peace" (Santi), etc.

In the *Udana* and *Itivuttaka*, the Buddha refers to *Nibbana* as follows:—

"There is, O Bhikkhus, an unborn (ajata), unoriginated (abhuta), unmade (akata) and non-conditioned state (asamkhata). If, O Bhikkhus, there were not this unborn, unoriginated, unmake and non-conditioned, an escape for the born, originated, made, and conditioned, would not be possible here. As there is an unborn, unoriginated, unmade and non-conditioned state, an escape for the born, originated, made, conditioned is possible."

The *Itivuttaka* states:

"The born, become, produced, compounded, made,
And thus not lasting, but of birth and death
An aggregate, a nest of sickness, brittle,
A thing by food supported, come to be,

'Twere no fit thing to take delight in such.
Th'escape therefrom, the real, beyond the sphere
Of reason, lasting, unborn, unproduced,
The sorrowless, the stainless path that ends.
The things of woe, the peace from worries, bliss."

The *Nibbana* of Buddhists is therefore, neither a state of nothingness nor a mere cessation. What it is not, one can definitely say. What precisely it is, one cannot adequately express in conventional terms as it is unique. It is for self-realization.

SOPADISESA AND ANUPADISESA NIBBANA DHATU

References are frequently made in the books to *Nibbana* as *Sopadisesa* and *Anupadisesa Nibbana Dhatu.*

These in fact are not two kinds of *Nibbana,* but the one single *Nibbana* receiving its name according to experience of it before and after death.

Nibbana is attainable in this present life itself if the seeker fits himself for it. Buddhism nowhere states that its ultimate goal can be reached only in a life beyond. Here lies the difference between the Buddhist conception of *Nibbana* and the non-Buddhist conception of an eternal heaven which is attainable only after death.

When *Nibbana* is realized in the body, it is called *Sopadisesa Nibbana Dhatu.* When an *Arahat* attains *Parinibbana* after the dissolution of the body, without any remainder of any physical existence, it is called *Anupadisesa Nibbana Dhatu.*

In the *Itivuttaka,* the Buddha says:

"There are, O Bhikkhus, two elements of *Nibbana* with the basis still remaining. Herein O Bhikkhus a Bhikkhu is an *Arahat,* one who has destroyed the Defilements who has lived the life, done what was to be done, laid aside the burden, who has attained his goal, who has destroyed the fetters of existence, who rightly understood, is delivered. His five sense-organs still remain and as he is not devoid of them he undergoes the pleasant and the unpleasant experiences. That destruction of his attachment, hatred and delusion is called 'the Element of *Nibbana* with the basis still remaining.'

"What, O Bhikkhus, is 'the Element of *Nibbana* without the basis"?

"Herein, O Bhikkhus, a Bhikkhu is an *Arahat*......is delivered. In this very life, all his sensations will have no delight for him, they will be cooled. This is called "the Element of *Nibbana* without a basis."

> "These two *Nibbana*-states are shown by Him
> Who seeth, who is such and unattached.
> One state is that in this same life possessed
> With base remaining, tho' becoming's stream
> Be cut off. While the state without a base
> Belongeth to the future, wherein all
> Becomings utterly do come to cease.
> They who, by knowing this state uncompounded
> Have heart's release, by cutting off the stream,
> They who have reached the core of Dhamma, glad
> To end, — such have abandoned all becomings."

CHARACTERISTICS OF NIBBANA

What is *Nibbana,* friend? The destruction of lust, the destruction of hatred, the destruction of delusion — that, friend, is called *Nibbana*.

Samyutta Nikaya

In contradistinction to Samsara, the phenomenal existence, *Nibbana* is eternal (dhuva), desirable (subha), and happy (sukha).

According to Buddhism all things, mundane and supramundane, are classified into two divisions, namely, those conditioned by causes (samkhata) and those not conditioned by any cause (asamkhata).

These three are the features of all conditioned things (Samkhatalakkhanani):— arising (uppada), cessation (vaya) and change of state (thitassa annathattam).

Arising or becoming is an essential characteristic of everything that is conditioned by a cause or causes. That which arises or becomes is subjected to change and dissolution. Every conditioned thing is constantly becoming and is perpetually changing. The universal law of change applies to everything in the cosmos — both mental and physical — ranging from the minutest germ or tiniest particle to the highest being or the most massive object. Mind, though imperceptible, changes faster even than matter.

Nibbana, a supramundane state, realized by Buddhas and Arahats, are declared to be not conditioned by any cause. Hence it is not subjected to any becoming, change and dissolution. It is birthless (ajata), decayless (ajara), and deathless (amara). Strictly speaking, *Nibbana* is neither a cause nor an effect. Hence it is unique (kevala).

Everything that has sprung from a cause must inevitably pass away, and as such is undesirable (asubha).

Life is man's dearest possession, but when he is confronted with insuperable difficulties and unbearable burdens, then that very life becomes an intolerable burden. Sometimes he tries to seek relief by putting an end to his life as if suicide would solve all his individual problems.

Bodies are adorned and adored. But those charming, adorable and enticing forms, when disfigured by time and disease, become extremely repulsive.

Men desire to live peacefully and happily with their near ones, surrounded by amusements and pleasures, but, if by some misfortune, the wicked world runs counter to their ambitions and desires, the inevitable sorrow is then almost indescribably sharp.

The following beautiful parable aptly illustrates the fleeting nature of life and its alluring pleasures.

A man was forcing his way through a thick forest beset with thorns and stones. Suddenly to his great consternation, an elephant appeared and gave chase. He took to his heels through fear, and, seeing a well, he ran to hide in it. But to his horror he saw a viper at the bottom of the well. However, lacking other means of escape, he jumped into the well, and clung to a thorny creepy that was growing in it.

Looking up, he saw two mice — a white and a black one — gnawing at the creeper. Over his face there was a beehive from which occasional drops of honey trickled.

This man, foolishly unmindful of this precarious position, was greedily tasting the honey. A kind person volunteered to show him a path of escape. But the greedy man begged to be excused till he had enjoyed himself.

The thorny path is *samsara*, the ocean of life. Man's life is not a bed of roses. It is beset with difficulties and obstacles to overcome, with opposition and unjust criticism, with attacks and insults to be borne. Such is the thorny path of life.

The elephant here resembles death; the viper, old age; the creeper, birth; the two mice, night and day. The drops of honey correspond to the fleeting sensual pleasures. The kind man is the Buddha.

The so-called material happiness is merely the gratification of some desire. When the desired thing is gained, another desire arises. Insatiate are all desires.

Sorrow is essential to life, and cannot be evaded. *Nibbana*, being non-conditioned, is eternal (dhuva), desirable (subha), and happy (sukha).

The happiness of *Nibbana* should be differentiated from ordinary worldly happiness. Nibbanic bliss grows neither stale nor monotonous. It is a form of happiness that never wearies, never fluctuates. It arises by allaying passions (vupasama) unlike that temporary worldly happiness which results from the gratification of some desire (vedayita).

In the *Bahuvedaniya Sutta,* the Buddha enumerates ten grades of happiness beginning with the gross material pleasures which result from the pleasant stimulation of the senses. As one ascends higher and higher in the moral plane, the type of happiness becomes ever more exalted, sublime and subtle, so much so that the world scarely recognizes it as happiness. In the first *Jhana,* one experiences a transcendental happiness (sukha), absolutely independent of the five senses. This happiness is realized by inhibiting the desire for the pleasures of the senses, highly prized by the materialist. In the forth *Jhana,* however, even this type of happiness is discarded as coarse and unprofitable, and equanimity (upekkha) is termed happiness.

The Buddha says:

"Fivefold, Ananda, are sensual bonds. What are the five forms cognizable by the eye — desirable, lovely, charming, infatuating, accompanied by thirst, and arousing the dust of the passions; sounds cognizable by the ear; odours cognizable by the nose; flavours cognizable by the tongue; contacts cognizable by the body — desirable, lovely charming, infatuating, accompanied by thirst. and arousing the dust of passions. These, Ananda, are the five sensual bonds. Whatever happiness or pleasures arises from these sensual bonds, is known as sensual happiness."

Who so should declare:— "This is the highest happiness and pleasure which beings may experience" — I do not grant him that, and why? Because there is other happiness more exalted and sublime.

And what is that other happiness more exalted and sublime? Here a Bhikkhu lives, completely separated from sense-

74

desires, remote from immoral states, with initial and sustained application born of seclusion, in joy and happiness, abiding in the First Ecstasy (Pathama Jhana). This is happiness more exalted and sublime.

But should anyone declare:— "This is the highest happiness and pleasure which beings may experience" — I do not grant him that, and why? Because there is another happiness yet more exalted and sublime.

Here a Bhikkhu, stilling initial and sustained application, having tranquility within, mind predominating, initial and sustained application having ceased, as a result of peace, lives in joy and happiness abiding in the Second Ecstasy (Dutiya Jhana). This is the other happiness more exalted and sublime.

Yet should anyone declare that this is the highest happiness and pleasure experienced by beings — I do not grant it. There is happiness more exalted.

Here a Bhikkhu from absence of desire for joy, abides serene, mindful, and completely conscious, experiencing in the body that of which the *Ariyas* says:— "Endowed with equanimity and mindfulness he abides in bliss." Thus he lives abiding in the Third Ecstasy (Tatiya Jhana). This is the other happiness and pleasure more exalted and sublime.

Still should anyone declare that this is the highest happiness — I do not grant it. There is happiness more exalted.

Here a Bhikkhu, abandoning pleasure and pain, leaving behind former joy and grief — painless, pleasureless, perfect in equanimity and mindfulness — lives abiding in the Fourth

Ecstasy (Catuttha Jhana). This is the other happiness more exalted and sublime.

However, were this declared to be the highest happiness — I do not grant it. There is happiness more sublime.

Here a Bhikkhu, passing entirely beyond the perception of form, with the disappearance of sense reaction, freed from attention to perceptions of diversity, thinks: 'Infinity is Space' and lives abiding in the Realm of Infinite Space (Akasanancayatana). This other happiness is more exalted and sublime.

Nevertheless, if this were declared the highest happiness — I do not grant it. There is happiness more sublime.

Here a Bhikkhu, transcending entirely the Realm of Infinite Space, thinks: 'Infinite is Consciousness' and lives abiding in the Realm of Infinite Consciousness (Vinnanancayatana). This other happiness is more exalted and sublime.

And yet should this be declared the highest happiness — I do not grant it. There is higher happiness.

Here a Bhikkhu, transcending the Realm of Infinite Consciousness, thinks: 'There is nothing whatsoever' and lives abiding in the Realm of Nothingness (Akincannayatana). This other happiness is more exalted and sublime than that.

And still were this declared the highest happiness — I do not grant it. There is happiness more exalted.

Here a Bhikkhu, passing entirely beyond the Realm of Nothingness, lives abiding in the Realm of Neither Perception nor Non-Perception (N'eva sanna N'asanna, yatana). This other happiness is more exalted and sublime.

Yet who so should declare:— "This is the highest bliss and pleasure which beings may experience" — I do not grant him that, and why? Because yet another happiness is more exalted and sublime.

And what is this other happiness more exalted and sublime? Here's a Bhikkhu, utterly transcending the Realm of Neither Perception nor Non-Perception, lives, having attained to the Cessation of Perception and Sensation (Sannavedayita — Nirodha). This, Ananda, is the other happiness more exalted and sublime.

Of all the ten grades of happiness this is the highest and the most sublime. This transcendental state is *Nirodha Samapatti,* that is, experiencing *Nibbana* in this life itself.

As the Buddha Himself has anticipated, one may ask: "How can that state be called highest happiness when there is no consciousness to experience it?"

The Buddha replies: "Nay, disciples, the Tathagata does not recognize bliss merely because of a pleasurable sensation, but disciples, wherever bliss is attained there and there only does the Accomplished One recognize bliss."

"I proclaim," says the Buddha, "that everything experienced by the senses is sorrow." But why? Because one in sorrow craves to be happy and the so-called happy crave to be happier still. So insatiate is worldly happiness.

In conventional terms the Buddha declares: *"Nibbanam*

paramam sukham — Nibbana is the highest bliss." It is bliss supreme because it is not a kind of happiness experienced by the senses. It is a blissful state of positive relief from the ills of life.

The very fact of the cessation of suffering is ordinarily termed happiness, though this is not an appropriate word to depict its real nature.

WHERE IS NIBBANA?

In the *Milinda Panha,* the Venerable Nagasena answers this question thus:

"There is no spot looking East, South, West, or North, above, below, or beyond, where *Nibbana* is situated and yet *Nibbana* is; and he who orders his life alright, grounded in virtue and with rational attention, may realize it whether he lives in Greece, China, Alexandra, or in Kosala."

"Just as fire is not stored up in any particular place but arises when the necessary conditions exist, so *Nibbana* is said not to exist in a particular place, but it is attained when the necessary conditions are fulfilled."

In the *Rohitassa Sutta,* the Buddha states: "In this very one fathom-long body, along with its perceptions and thoughts do I proclaim the world, the origin of the world, the cessation of the world and the path leading to the cessation of the world."

Here world means suffering. The cessation of the world, therefore, means the cessation of suffering which is *Nibbana.*

One's *Nibbana* is dependent upon this one-fathom body. It is not something that is created nor is it something to be created.

Nibbana is there where the four elements of cohesion (apo), extension (pathavi), heat (tejo) and motion (vayo) find no footing.

Referring to where *Nibbana* is, *Samyutta Nikaya* states:—

> "Where the four elements that cleave, and stretch,
> And burn, and move no further footing find."

In the *Udana*, the Buddha says:

"Just as, O Bhikkhus, notwithstanding those rivers that reach the great ocean and the torrents of rain that fall from the sky, neither a deficit nor a surplus is perceptible in the great ocean, even so despite the many Bhikkhus that enter the remainderless *Parinibbana*, there is neither a deficit nor a surplus in the element of *Nibbana*."

Nibbana is, therefore, not a kind of heaven where a transcendental ego resides, but a Dhamma (an attainment) which is within the reach of us all.

An eternal heaven, which provides all forms of pleasures desired by man and where one enjoys happiness to one's heart's content, is practically inconceivable. It is absolutely impossible to think that such a place could exist permanently anywhere.

Granting that there is no place where *Nibbana* is stored up, King Milinda questions Venerable Nagasena whether there is any basis whereon a man stand and, ordering his life aright, realize *Nibbana*.

"Yes, O King, there is such a basis."

"Which, then Venerable Nagasena, is that basis?"

"Virtue, O King, is that basis. For, if grounded in virtue, and careful in attention, whether in the land of the Scythians or the Greeks, whether in China or in Tartary, whether in Alexandria or in Nikumba, whether in Benares or in Kosala, whether in Kashmir or in Gandhara, whether on a mountain top or in the highest heavens, — wherever he may be, the man who orders his life aright will attain *Nibbana*."

WHAT ATTAINS NIBBANA?

This question must necessarily be set aside as irrelevant, for Buddhism denies the existence of a permanent entity or an immortal soul.

The so-called being of which we often hear as the vestment of the soul is a mere bundle of conditioned factors.

The Arahat Bhikkhuni Vajira says:

"And just when the parts are rightly set,
The work 'chariot' ariseth (in our minds).
So doth our usage covenant to say,
A being when the aggregates are there."

According to Buddhism, the so-called being consists of mind and matter (nama-rupa) which constantly change with lightning rapidity. Apart from these two composite factors there exists no permanent soul or an unchanging entity. The so-called "I" is also an illusion.

Instead of an eternal soul or an illusory 'I', Buddhism posits a dynamic life-flux (santati) which bows and infinitum as long as it is fed with ignorance and craving. When these two root causes are eradicated by any individual on attaining Arahatship, they cease to flow with his final death.

In conventional terms, one says that the *Arahat* has attained *Parinibbana* or passed away into *Nibbana*.

"As right now, and here" there is neither a permanent ego nor an identical being it is needless to state that there can be no 'I' or a soul (atta) in *Nibbana*.

The *Visuddhi Magga* states:—

> "Misery only doth exist, none miserable
> Nor doer is there, nought save the deed is found
> *Nibbana* is, but not the man who seeks it
> The path exists, but not the traveller on it."

The chief difference between the Buddhist conception of *Nibbana* and the Hindu conception of *Nibbana* or *Mukti* lies in the fact that Buddhists view their goal without an eternal soul and creator, while Hindus do believe in an eternal soul and a creator.

This is the reason why Buddhism can neither be called Eternalism nor Nihilism.

In *Nibbana,* nothing is eternalised nor is anything annihilated. ·

As Sir Edwin Arnold says:—

> "If any teach *Nibbana* is to cease,
> Say unto such they lie.
> If any teach *Nibbana* is to live,
> Say unto such they err."

82

It must be admitted that this question of *Nibbana* is the most difficult in the Teaching of the Buddha. However much we may speculate we shall never be in a position to comprehend its real nature. The best way to understand *Nibbana* is to try to realize it with our own intuitive knowledge.

Although *Nibbana* cannot be perceived by the five senses and lies in obscurity in so far as the average man is concerned, the only straight path that leads to *Nibbana* has been explained by the Buddha with all the necessary details and is laid open to all. The goal is now clouded, but the method of achievement is perfectly clear and when that achievement is realized, the Goal is as clear as 'the moon freed from clouds'.
